## Twilight's Soft Return

When twilight slips in, the shadows take flight,
I grab a good book for a giggly night.
Characters cackle, conspiracies abound,
As I laugh with the stories time has draped round.

Out on the swing, oh what a delight,
With crickets a-singing, they join the night.
A ghost of a squirrel flits by with a grin,
Dip into laughter, let the fun times begin!

The stars peek like children, curious and bright,
As I wave to the moon, it gives me a light.
With secrets and jokes on the porch steps I see,
The night quakes with laughter, annoyance set free.

So here's to the twilight, a soft, chuckled tune,
Where laughter dances nightly beneath the bright moon.
With every tick-tock, all worries unfurl,
The magic of moments brings joy to our world.

## **A Frame of Old Photographs**

Snap! A picture taken long ago,
They're hanging on walls, but they're putting on a show.
Granny with a beehive, oh what a sight!
In polka-dot dresses that twirled with delight.

Uncle Joe's covered in what looks like cake,
Trying to impress with a big fish he'll fake.
Cousins we knew had hair like hay,
Laughing together in a chaotic bouquet.

The frames all chuckle, sharing their lore,
Of wild family parties and good food galore.
A dance in the kitchen, a spill on the floor,
As memories linger, who could ask for more?

So we gather around, let the photos relive,
The funny old stories that they long to give.
Perhaps we're the punchline that time has adored,
A frame full of laughter, oh how we soared!

## Secrets Beneath the Floorboards

What lies beneath where we rarely peek?
Old bones of secrets and dust that squeak.
A shoe from a dancer, perhaps a lost sock,
That time had forgotten, now part of the block.

My grandpa's old jokes, they creak with the beams,
Whispering laughter in dusty daydreams.
A riddle left buried, beneath the old floor,
Where ticklish toes danced 'til they couldn't no more.

The ghosts of my childhood, piled high like a heap,
Scribbled notes and old toys, all perfectly steep.
I poke with a stick, hear a giggle or two,
Wondering what mischief they'd get up to.

So let's pry up the boards, let the secrets unwind,
A treasure of memories, a gold mine we find.
With each crack and creak, a chuckle we yield,
As the whispers of time lose their hesitant shield.

## Ghosts of Old Footfalls

In shadows where the echoes dance,
I swear I saw a poltergeist prance.
It wiggled its toes, and I nearly squealed,
As it rummaged 'round for some old revealed.

The creaks above made me glance up,
Perhaps a specter sipping from a chipped cup?
With a wink and a nod, it vanished away,
Leaving me giggling at ghosts that play.

My cat looked startled, jumped in fright,
As old memories fluttered, dancing in light.
We shared some laughs at the silliness there,
While the walls whispered stories they'd love to share.

So here's to the fun, the silly, the glee,
Of spirits that visit for tea, not to flee.
In the stillness of night, let them drift and sway,
For life's just a party—it's here to stay.

## The Rattle of the Screen Door

The screen door squeaks like a tickled old friend,
Every time it rattles, our laughter won't end.
It tells of our antics, our joy and our strife,
In a symphony of chaos, it celebrates life.

Cousins run in, dragging mud on the floor,
While Aunty shouts, "Who's tracking in more?"
The rattle rings out as we race to the fridge,
What's better than snacks? A light-hearted bridge.

A dog bolts by, tail wagging with cheer,
The rattle grows louder, it's music we hear.
Old jokes resurface, they dance in the room,
With each squeaky jiggle, there's laughter to bloom.

As sunset approaches, the door sings its tune,
Bringing us back to the warmth of the moon.
In this rattling rhythm, our hearts find repose,
With fond memories swirling like petals of prose.

## Lanterns in the Late Hour

In the twilight glow, laughter spills like wine,
Lanterns dance lightly, coaxing tales divine.
Ghosts of the past peek in with a grin,
As we share the stories, where do I begin?

Grandpa recalls the time he fell in a pool,
With a splash and a gasp, what a foolish rule!
The night is alive with our silly exchanges,
Under each lantern, humor rearranges.

Mismatched socks twinkle like stars in the night,
Uncle Joe trips and gives quite a fright.
But he stands up grinning, dusts off his pride,
We burst into laughter, with joy as our guide.

As evening deepens, our antics increase,
Every lantern a witness, every giggle a feast.
In the glow of the night, we're forever young,
With lanterns above, our songs are well sung.

## Sipping Time's Sweet Nectar

Lemonade spills from a jug on the floor,
Mom's face turns red, we all laugh and roar.
Sugar rush hits, and our giggles ignite,
As we sip away memories, oh what a sight!

With each sunny sip, tales bubble and brew,
Of fireflies dancing and a dog that once flew.
Mismatched socks and forgotten shoes,
Life's little blunders become our good news.

We swap silly stories that lighten the load,
Like my uncle's mishap with an oversized toad.
As laughter erupts, and we're lost in the haze,
Sipping sweet nectar, we're swept in a daze.

Memories flow as the sun sets low,
With each silly episode, our hearts grow and glow.
Toasting to moments, both silly and bright,
Sipping the sweet time, oh what a delight!

## The Wind Tells Tales

Whispers of laughter float on air,
Stories of clumsy folks everywhere.
The breeze nudges me, full of glee,
As it recounts my past, oh so funny!

A cat chased a squirrel, each one a blur,
With a leap and a twist, what a humorous stir!
They tumbled and rolled in a fanciful dance,
While I watched and chuckled, lost in a trance.

Old rocking chairs squeak like they know,
Tales of my youth, put on quite the show.
As wind swirls around, the tales unfold,
In this gentle breeze, old jesters are bold.

Each gust brings a chuckle, each rustle a grin,
Echoes of laughter, where the fun begins.
The wind plays the jester, a playful old chap,
Reminding me always to take life with a clap.

## Dialogues with Distant Dreams

In the attic, time stands still,
Each box whispers, gives a thrill.
Tufts of dust start to conspire,
Echoes of dreams to rehire.

We danced with shadows, held our breath,
Imagined treasures beyond death.
Our capes were blankets, fierce and bold,
Fighting dragons not yet told.

Laughing late with half-closed eyes,
We drew our worlds, painted the skies.
Riding bikes that flew too high,
To kingdoms only we could spy.

Now we talk to those young seeds,
Watering their wildest needs.
With every chuckle, every scheme,
We gossip with those distant dreams.

## Lanterns Lit in the Night of Memory

When lanterns flicker, shadows play,
Old stories come out to sway.
We light them up with laughter bright,
Chasing echoes of moonlit night.

The creaky swing still calls my name,
As if to tease me, play the game.
Ghosts of laughter, flickered light,
Whispers of youth, making things right.

Socks thrown high in joyful fights,
Pumpkin carving on chill nights.
With clay faces that never change,
We drew our dreams, a little strange.

Under stars, our secrets shared,
In wobbly boats, we were unprepared.
Now the night holds joyful gleam,
Those lanterns giggle in our dream.

# Heartbeats of Yesterday

Old photos stacked in dusty drawers,
Faces peeking, oh, the wars!
Toothless grins and crazy hats,
Was that really how we sat?

Bikes with wheels that squeaked and squealed,
Who knew that luck could be concealed?
A secret stash of candy bars,
Trading smiles beneath the stars.

Hiccups shared on summer days,
Silly stories, wild displays.
We swore we'd never grow up fast,
Oh, how those dreams have barely passed.

Now we giggle at our youth,
Crafting memories, a funny truth.
With heartbeats skipping through the years,
We'll find the joy and shed the tears.

# Chasing Shadows from Bygone Days

In the garden where we'd play,
Old toys rust and drift away.
A kite stuck high among the trees,
Faded laughter floats on the breeze.

We wore mismatched socks with pride,
Chased the ice cream truck, we'd hide.
With sticky fingers, sweet and red,
We ran until the daylight fled.

The treehouse swayed like ships at sea,
Worn-out dreams of daring free.
Ropes frayed, yet we climbed so high,
Pretended we could touch the sky.

Now we stroll and share our tales,
Forget our worries; laugh, it sails.
Like shadows danced in fading light,
Our childish joy takes flight tonight.

## **Swaying in the Arms of Memory**

Kites and balloons drift far away,
A dance with the clouds in playful ballet.
Backyard sketches with crayons in hand,
Masterpieces made, but never quite grand.

A dog with a hat joins in the fun,
Chasing his tail, we all start to run.
Yelling 'catch me' as shadows grow long,
Mixed up tunes become our song.

Frogs on lily pads with crowns on their heads,
Ruling the pond where giggles are spread.
Tickles and hugs, an afternoon churn,
Swaying in laughter, forever we'll yearn.

Old stories swirl like leaves in the breeze,
Stirring our hearts with memories that tease.
Captured in time, forever to stay,
In the arms of our youth, where we all play.

## Sunlit Days Beneath a Rusty Roof

A chair creeks tales of off-key songs,
And feet tapping rhythms where everyone belongs.
Light filters in through cracked old panes,
Embracing the goofiness in our veins.

Bugs in their jammies, on the table they feast,
While ants march proudly, they're always the least.
Kettle whistling mostly just for show,
Filling the air with steam and woe.

Grandma's old quilt, a patchwork delight,
Holding secrets of warmer nights.
Noisy cicadas create such a ruckus,
Singing their ballads, oh, what a circus!

Under the rust, dreams skitter and glide,
A funny parade where memories reside.
We sip lemonade, toast to the past,
With glimpses of joy, forever amassed.

## **Tangled Roots of Yester-Morn**

Worms in the garden, plotting their scheme,
With lettuce hats, they weave and dream.
A cat named Whiskers, bold and proud,
Danced like a fool, drawing a crowd.

Swinging on vines, we made a mess,
Climbing too high, what a distress!
Ripe summer peaches, all squished and smushed,
Sticky giggles, as nature blushed.

Old photographs, a colorful blend,
Faded smiles that never quite end.
Mom's hairdos towering at sky-high,
Trust me, they're proof we dared to fly!

With popcorn showers from oaks in bloom,
We danced in circles, creating a room.
Whispers from roots, tangled and spry,
Echoes of laughter as time wanders by.

## Remembrances Carried on Soft Whispers

Old shoes left behind, what a sight!
They squeak with laughter, pure delight.
Ghosts of picnics, crumbs and cake,
Chasing the bees, oh, what a mistake!

Grandpa's jokes, they never age,
Dancing like clowns, up on the stage.
Stories of cats that stole his socks,
Oh, the chaos of mismatched clocks!

Memories flutter like leaves in breeze,
Tickling our hearts, they tease and please.
We gather 'round, eyes wide in glee,
As laughter spills like a playful spree.

The echoes chatter, a silly tune,
With every glance, we swoon and croon.
We sip from cups that never run dry,
Wrapped in the warmth of days gone by.

## **Remnants of Summer's Embrace**

The sun drips golden on faded old chairs,
While fireflies twinkle like little light flares.
A frisbee lies lonely, sad as a shoe,
With stories stuck in its plastic, who knew?

The dog's in a tangle with a ball and a sock,
While we swap our secrets, the ticking clock.
Each joke a treasure, each pun a delight,
As laughter unfolds in the soft twilight.

A patchwork of memories sewn into the air,
Where each moment shared is a little bit rare.
The summer days fade, but the fun stays alive,
With echoes of joy that always will thrive!

So here, in this corner, we gather our cheer,
With remnants around us, we relive our career.
For nothing compares to this whimsical space,
Where giggles and memories dance with grace!

## Echoes of Forgotten Laughter

In the corner, a radio plays an old tune,
As we stomp our feet to the beat of a moon.
The memories shimmy like moths in the night,
With echoes of laughter that feel just right!

A lopsided swing sings a creaking refrain,
While a pair of old sandals enjoy the terrain.
The garden gnomes witness all of our bliss,
With smiles so wide, they could not be amiss!

Each sunset gathers our funny little charms,
From dramatic fall to overswept arms.
We honor the moments, with hiccups galore,
As we share our adventures, eager for more!

With shadows adancing, the fun will not cease,
For memories linger and never find peace.
Here's to the smiles and the tales we share best,
In this echoing laughter, we're surely blessed!

## Shadows Caught in Time

Under the porch light, the shadows convene,
Elders arguing over who laughed too mean.
With wobbly chairs, we plan our next scheme,
As giggles erupt like a bubbling stream.

A ghostly old clock ticks a rhythm of cheer,
While crickets join in with a soundtrack to hear.
A lost tennis ball rolls over to play,
It's been on a journey, or so they say!

The stories unfold in a hiccuping tone,
Of chickens who danced and the dog who blewn.
As shadows flicker and stories blend,
Laughter's the thread that will never end!

So here we all sit, in a world spun with jest,
Trading our tales like we're on a quest.
In the light of a past that refuses to fade,
We find joy in the mishaps and wild escapades.

## Whispers of Rustling Leaves

In a creaky chair, the tales are spun,
Of squirrels playing hide and seek in the sun.
My old dog snores with a wheezy delight,
Chasing dreams of mailmen, oh what a sight!

The wind tickles my nose with a giggling breeze,
While shadows dance under the swaying trees.
I swear that old cat just winked at a shoe,
And the raccoon's still plotting his midnight coup!

Grandma's old hat is now quite the crown,
When worn by the child who spins round and brown.
The neighbors peek in, all wide-eyed and grinning,
As I slip and trip, oh, what a beginning!

Oh, memories are stitched in chipped wooden beams,
With laughter that sparkles like wild, fleeting dreams.
A gathering of moments, both silly and sweet,
Where life's little quirks are the gift of our seat.

## Blue Sky Collage of Dreams

Up high, a plane trails a line,
We point and wish it's all divine.
Clouds like sheep, soft and white,
Tumble into our silly flight.

A kite tangles in a tree,
Laughs erupt, oh so carefree.
Naps are taken on the grass,
While daisies cheer as we pass.

With popcorn kernels stuck in hair,
We giggle sweet without a care.
Chasing shadows as they grow,
Inviting whimsy with each flow.

As daylight fades to a hum,
In starlit dreams, we all become.
A wild collage up above,
Painted with laughter, joy, and love.

## In the Shade of Remembering

Under the tree, we share our lore,
With ice cream drips we can't ignore.
A twig fight leads to squeaky screams,
As we hatch up our wildest dreams.

Tattered comics on the ground,
Adventures of heroes long renowned.
Superheroes in our heads,
Flying high above our beds.

Bubbles float like visions grand,
Cat tails swat at what we planned.
Old toys cast aside in glee,
Together, just you, just me.

Voices bounce like echoes loud,
Forgetting worries in our crowd.
In the shade where laughter rings,
We create our own magic flings.

## Hues of Autumnal Remembrance

Leaves tumble down like clumsy fools,
Wearing hats made of the school rules.
Pumpkins grin from every spot,
While cider spills in a joyful plot.

Sweaters fuzzy, not too tight,
We dance 'round bonfires at night.
Ghost stories spun with flair and fun,
Then run like mad when the tale is done!

Corn mazes lead to giggles loud,
Where lost kids huddle, feeling proud.
A scarecrow mocks with a crooked smile,
As we munch on snacks, righteous and vile.

Hot cocoa spills down my chin,
Chocolate mustaches—I win!
With autumn's hues all around,
Our laughter is the sweetest sound.

## Bone and Bark of Heritage

Old chairs creak with tales to share,
A cat naps without a care.
Mismatched socks on a line,
Grandma swears they were once fine.

Lemonade spills on the floor,
Who needs carpets? We roar!
Each wood knot tells a joke,
While the wind joins in with a poke.

The dog rolls in dirt with glee,
A muddy print just for me.
Flip-flops offer a sweet dance,
As squirrels steal their chance to prance.

A hammock swinging side to side,
We giggle at the world outside.
With cupcakes perched on the rail,
We laugh as old stories prevail.

## The Silent Witness

The old swing creaks, a guardian gray,
Of childhood antics from yesterday.
It watched us fly, then tumble down,
From awkward moments to our silly crown.

One minute we're young, then it's all a blur,
As we push and laugh, looking to stir.
"Higher!" we'd yell, with hearts full of glee,
The swing just grinned, oh so carefree.

Now it rocks slow in the midday sun,
Holding secrets of how we had fun.
Like a time capsule, it guards each prank,
With echoes of laughter in every plank.

Though years have flown, here it remains,
A witness to joy, our growing pains.
With chipped paint and knots that cling tight,
The silent witness of laughter's light.

## **Voices of Distant Summers**

Echoes of laughter on sun-kissed days,
With fireflies dancing in whimsical ways.
"Who ate the ice cream?" a shrill voice cried,
As sticky fingers showed where we tried.

The hammock swayed with tales of old,
Of monsters beneath beds, so bold.
We'd tell ghost stories, then run like the wind,
During those summers when no one pinned.

Each laugh a note in the memory's tune,
Like chasing the stars on a bright summer's moon.
With lemonade sips, and sweet sunburns,
Our youthful days held endless turns.

So I sit back, listen close to the breeze,
With whispers of summers that tease and please.
Their voices echo still, with giggles that swell,
In the heart of this moment where memories dwell.

**Fading Footprints on the Threshold**


Footprints fade, a merry chase,
In the dirt where we ran with grace.
A hop, skip, and jump to the old oak tree,
Where squirrels plot to outsmart me.

Each shoe tells a story of mud and fun,
While I roll my eyes at all we've done.
"Did you just fall?" they snickered in glee,
As I landed hard, 'Oh, woe is me!'

But with scraped knees, I kept up the pace,
While laughter echoed in that wild place.
Now footprints linger, but the tales remain,
Of mischief and joy, not a hint of pain.

So here I stand, at the threshold wide,
With follies behind that I cannot hide.
Each step a reminder, so silly, so spry,
Of youth's grand adventure beneath the sky.

## A Chair with a View


In the old chair, it creaks and sighs,
Waiting for stories from goofy lies.
A bird lands, gives a cheeky nod,
As I sip tea, feeling quite odd.

Neighbors pass with their tales to share,
Like the cat who thinks it's got flair.
I chuckle and wave, but not too loud,
For the chair is a part of the crowd.

Memories dance, but can't quite please,
Like socks that vanish in the breeze.
With each glance, I see their kin,
In the chair where laughter's been.

So I rock back, on this front-line chair,
With the world below, without a care.
For each creak tells me of days gone by,
When all we did was laugh and sigh.

**Moments Wrapt in Melancholy**

In whispers of dusk, the stories unwind,
Laughter and lessons so tenderly twined.
The clock struck its chime, and we tumbled in time,
Catchy old jingles, so silly, yet prime!

Old chairs creak their secrets, from years gone by,
While trying to stand tall, and not say goodbye.
A cake made of carrots, we dared to devour,
Left us quite giddy, oh what a power!

Filling the room with the smell of our past,
Like fruitcake endeavors that never held fast.
Yet in all the giggles, a hint of sweet sighs,
Moments wrapped soft, like a low-flying prize.

## **Footsteps on the Path of Reminiscence**

On narrow old pathways, our feet weave a song,
Hiccups of humor, where all could go wrong.
The kite that got stuck in old Mister Brown's tree,
It pulled all our laughter, but gave us a spree!

A dog dressed as pirate, a parrot to boot,
Captured the heart of the neighborhood's loot.
Like socks paired with sandals, such fashion delight,
Making waves of confusion, in the morning light.

Pillows in castles, we built high in the air,
Friendly debates on the merits of flair.
As we strolled down the lane, those echoes still sing,
In steps filled with joy, those moments we cling.

## **Comfort from a Shaded Past**

Beneath branches wide, with a swing that's a wreck,
Stories come pouring, like rain on a deck.
Uncle's wild antics, a parade of the strange,
Like that time at the barbecue, oh what a change!

The lemonade's sour, but it brings back delight,
A picnic of chaos, from noon until night.
A squirrel in a top hat, just getting its groove,
Swaying to music, while we all try to move!

Cookie recipes lost in the depths of a drawer,
With flour explosions, the house became lore.
The moments we cherished, their warmth in the shade,
Mix laughter with joy, and the memories made.

## Twilight's Embrace of Old Secrets

In the evening glow, tales come to play,
Grandma's wild stories, they brighten the day.
A raccoon in the garden, our treasure hunt's prize,
Turns out to be nothing, just last week's fries!

The cat told a joke, or so we believed,
With a flick of her tail, we all got deceived.
Old photos of dancing, our moves full of flair,
Yet none of us knew how to manage our hair!

We laughed at the blunders, the slip-ups brand new,
Like Uncle Joe's socks that just never quite grew.
In twilight's embrace, our secrets unwind,
Fabric of laughter, with memories aligned.

## **Steps to Yesterday**

Old steps creak tales of those who went past,
Each footfall echoes in a delightful cast.
Squeaky swings call with a voice so sweet,
Remembering summers of sticky bare feet.

Hopscotch lines faded, but oh what a game!
We leaped and we laughed for glory and fame.
Our shouts filled the air, with giggles and squeals,
Daring each other with wild, silly deals.

Marbles and jacks scattered across the yard,
Our childhood heroes, all fought and scarred.
A slingshot in hand, dreams aimed with delight,
Innocent mischief made everything right.

With every step taken, the past brings a grin,
Those moments return, let the laughter begin!
We dance through the echoes, both old and anew,
On steps that remember the antics we drew.

## Stories Woven in Twilight

Twilight settles like a soft, warm blanket,
Stories emerge, like secrets from a trinket.
Granny spins yarns, gold sparkles in her eye,
While we roll our eyes, just waiting to sigh.

The tales of the past, both silly and bold,
Of fashion mistakes, oh, the laughter retold!
She wore purple pants with polka dots bright,
We burst into giggles at her wild sight.

In each whispered tale, we chuckle and snort,
How Uncle Lou danced like he played in a sport.
With every quip and each clumsy romance,
We gather in laughter, all under the trance.

As stars peek out in the indigo sky,
We reminisce as the night passes by.
Woven in laughter, our hearts intertwine,
With each funny story, the joy is divine.

**Nostalgic Skies Above**

Clouds drift lazily, a whimsical show,
Their fluffy formations steal the glow.
We gaze up in awe, pointing with glee,
At a stegosaurus, then a giant bee!

Kites from our childhood get tangled in trees,
Each gust of wind brings silly unease.
We stumble and trip like we used to do,
Laughter erupts, for we're friends, not few.

The ice cream truck's tune brings back sunny days,
Of sticky fingers and syrupy ways.
We recount the flavors and funny old schemes,
Laughing till we burst at our silly ice dreams.

Underneath skies where the echoes still play,
We find joy in the echoes, come what may.
With laughter and love writing stories so grand,
In the light of the past, we proudly stand.

## **Sunlight Through the Cracks**

Sunlight spills in, a lively dance,
Old chairs creak with a jolly chance.
Sneaky shadows chase the dust,
Faded memories, a funny must.

A cat sprawls out, it's quite the sight,
Chasing beams in a nap-induced fight.
The radio crackles, tunes from the past,
A funny tune, how long will they last?

Jars of lemonade, sweetened just right,
Grandpa spills stories that tickle the night.
We giggle and snort at his silly ways,
All while the sunlight begins to blaze.

Laughter echoes through chipped wooden beams,
As the world outside fades into dreams.
We toast to the moments, both quirky and bright,
In this lively place, we always unite.

## Graceful Aging of the Seasons

In autumn's glow, the leaves would dance,
Like old folks at a ball.
We twirled and spun in pure romance,
With laughter, heedless, all.

The winter chill brought snowballs tight,
Thrown at neighbors, what a game!
But hitting dad was pure delight,
And brought him so much shame.

Spring bloomed forth with colors bright,
We jumped in puddles deep.
The flowers, though a fragrant sight,
Gave bees a chance to creep.

Summer lingered, lazy days,
With ice cream drips and cheer.
We'd laugh about our silly ways,
As years just disappeared.

# Remnants of a Sunlit Childhood

Underneath the old oak tree,
We built our castles high.
With sticks and stones, oh what a spree,
We aimed for the blue sky.

The cookies burnt, we tried to bake,
A recipe gone wrong.
The fire alarms, a great mistake,
Yet still we sang our song.

Our bikes were squeaky, tires flat,
But we raced with pure delight.
Each tumble felt, a careful spat,
Made every fall feel right.

Now those days seem distant, strange,
Yet laughter echoes still.
The crazy games, the silly range,
Have shaped us with a thrill.

## **Gazing at Faded Horizons**

With floppy hats and funny shoes,
We danced upon the lawn.
The neighbors stared and looked bemused,
At our impromptu dawn.

A kite that soared up to the skies,
Would swoop and flop right down.
My brother, with his goofy cries,
Spoke often of a crown.

The flowers wore bizarre perfume,
From mom's odd gardening spree.
The daisies gathered in full bloom,
Declared they'd set us free.

With stories spun and laughter grand,
We painted life with glee.
Who knew that simple, silly band,
Would form our family tree?

## Threads Woven in Time

In a chair that squeaks with age,
I sit with tales unwritten.
Grandma's stories, full of gage,
Turned out to be quite smitten.

My socks are mismatched on the floor,
I swear they hide and play.
An old cat's snoring is a roar,
As I reminisce all day.

The photographs, a tangly mess,
Of hats that were quite frumpy.
My hair in curls, I must confess,
I looked like a ruffled dumpy.

Yet laughter weaves through every seam,
Time's fabric, slightly tattered.
Each memory, a vibrant dream,
Where nothing much quite mattered.

## **Vignettes of the Forgotten**

In dusty corners, stories reside,
With comic relief that we can't hide.
A lady in lace claims she once could sing,
But all that comes out is a flat, funny ring.

Old bikes lean against the wall's side,
Each rusty pedal has tales to confide.
They remember the races, the falls, the scrapes,
Winning with flair, or just changing shapes.

A clock ticks away, counting moments so grand,
'If only I could totally understand!'
I tapped its face, it frowned back at me,
'It's time for laughter, can't you see?'

With echoes of giggles, these vignettes delight,
As faint glimmers flicker like stars in the night.
So raise a toast to the tales we find,
In forgotten corners, laughter unconfined.

## Timeless Tales of Sunlight

Sunlight winks through cracks in the wall,
Whispers of laughter, a beckoning call.
Old hats are flapping, stuck up on shelves,
Who knew they held dreams of forgotten elves?

Rumors abound of the socks on the floor,
Each one a story, no one can ignore.
Uncle Bob lost one in a shuffle so grand,
Now it's a legend, passed hand to hand.

There's a rocking chair that's seen it all,
Squeaks of wisdom, echoes that enthrall.
'I've rocked each child to dreamland's embrace',
Said it to me with a smile on its face.

Timeless moments hang in the air,
With giggles and warmth, beyond compare.
Each beam of sunlight, a mischievous sprite,
Playing a game of hide and delight.

## **Behind the Screen Door**

Behind the door, the chatter does swirl,
Of Aunt Edna and her latest twirl.
She claims she's spry, still throwing her hat,
But sits with tea, and a loaf of cat.

There's Uncle Joe, in a paper-thin chair,
Telling tales of how he beat a bear.
We all laugh hard at his twisted plot,
'You shouldn't fish if you can't catch a lot!'

The dog snoozes, dreaming of bones,
While kids are outside, yelling on phones.
'What time is dinner?' they always shout,
'Just eat your snacks, or be out of the scout!'

And when it rains, the stories pour in,
Like Grandma's yarns from a day back when.
We giggle and gasp at how it could be,
Life flip-flopping in sweet reverie.

## Conversations with Ghosts of Yesterday

I asked the ghost, did you ever dance?
She laughed and said, only in a trance.
I tripped on air, she floated right by,
   She's got moves, I can't even try.

We chatted 'bout the days of old style,
She wore a gown, big enough for a mile.
I told her jeans make me feel so spry,
She winked and said, 'Just give it a try.'

We reminisced about the wild town fairs,
Where folks would flirt without any cares.
I raised my drink, but hers was a ghost,
Echoes of laughter always seem to boast.

As twilight fell, the shadows grew keen,
She vanished fast, like she was never seen.
But I still hear her giggles in the air,
Haunting my dreams with a style to share.

## Textures of Remembrance

Each wrinkle tells a joke well-worn,
Through laughter shared, not forlorn.
Faded fabrics, a patchwork tale,
Of funny moments that never fail.

Jars of marbles, a colorful crowd,
Where mischief thrived, and laughter loud.
A cookie recipe with crumbs of glee,
That never turns out, but who's to agree?

The chairs all creak a woodsy cheer,
While slipping grandma shares a beer.
Every spill's a funny scene,
It's all in love; it's never mean.

So welcome the moments that time forgot,
With plenty of chuckles and sardonic wit.
In this cozy nest of silly blends,
Textures of remembrance, laughter sends.

## Harmony of Gentle Reverie

When twilight whispers, laughter drifts,
Among the soft, nostalgic gifts.
An old dog snores with dreams of chase,
While memories dance, a merry race.

The little ones tumble, their giggles soar,
As grandpa shows them the echoing lore.
A sock puppet jokes in a child's hand,
As stories wrap in a smiley band.

Bicycles rust on the path outside,
With tires popped, they've nowhere to ride.
Each dingy frame holds a glorious spark,
Of adventurous trips from dawn till dark.

Let dreams convene in the evening's light,
Where silly whispers make wrongs feel right.
In the gallery of smiles and glee,
Harmony rests in our reverie.

## The Weight of Worn-out Stories

In a corner, tales reside,
With bits of truth the jokes provide.
A tale of woe, a hair-raising feat,
That somehow ends with a rubbery treat.

The old lady claims she flew one day,
With a broomstick that led her astray.
Her friends all snicker, elbows in ribs,
While arguing if frogs really do fib.

Afternoons melt, and fishing lines tangle,
With every hook, a new tale dangles.
Old shoes fashioned into boat sails,
As laughter stirs up the heartfelt gales.

So spin the yarns, let laughter thrive,
In the weight of stories, we come alive.
For every fumble, every mistake,
Is a reason to giggle, for friendship's sake.

## Hints of Laughter in Cool Shadows

In cool shadows, giggles blend,
As memories chase around the bend.
A rocking chair creaks its tune,
While crickets join, a goofy swoon.

Old cats nap on the rickety stairs,
Dreaming of fish and playful flares.
The old man chuckles, a wise old sage,
At tales of youth, an endless page.

Dusty pictures hang with pride,
Of hairstyles gone and mismatched strides.
A family mixture, a kooky blend,
With every laugh that we commend.

So let us gather, share a grin,
At stories where the laughs begin.
In these shadows that never part,
Laughter echoes, a joyful art.

## **Snatches of Old Melodies**

A banjo twangs, off-key at best,
Frogs join in, quite the jest.
A squirrel dances, tail a blur,
In this patch of green, life's a stir.

Whistles echo, the wind does tease,
Crows cawing, holding their ease.
Sunshine spills on wooden floors,
As memories knock upon the doors.

A rickety table holds so much charm,
With scratches and spills, it's found its balm.
Old records spin tales of glee,
In tune with laughter, wild and free.

So gather 'round, let's sing aloud,
With every strum, we're unbowed.
In snatches of sound, the past comes clear,
With chuckles that dance, we find our cheer.

**A Rest for Wandering Thoughts**

The hammock sways, thoughts take flight,
As sunbeams dance, dreaming bright.
A bee buzzes with so much pride,
In this lazy nook, I've nothing to hide.

Socks mismatched, a fashion sin,
Old rubber boots, where do I begin?
The garden gnome, with hands on hips,
Chortles at my tangled trips.

Butterflies flutter, jobs undone,
Chasing the day, oh what fun!
Sipping lemonade, sunshine sweet,
With giggles ripe, life feels complete.

Clouds shaped like dogs drift overhead,
With every whim, mischief is bred.
Here in this world, I take my pause,
For wandering thoughts, I'm filled with awe.

## Cracked Memories and Timeless Sighs

Rusty swings, a crooked view,
Hints of laughter, whispers blue.
A juice box spills, a sticky grin,
Remnants of summer, where to begin?

Old photographs with faces bright,
Eyelids heavy, tucked in tight.
A stinky sneaker tossed on the floor,
Each whiff's a story, can't ignore.

Tea kettle sings a raucous tune,
Under the watchful eye of the moon.
An empty chair holds all the yesterdays,
In the glow of dusk, their spirit stays.

Chickens cluck a funny beat,
As time spins on, and we repeat.
With smiles and snickers, we embrace,
In cracked memories, we find our place.

## A Symphony of Whispers

In the corner, tales collide,
With squeaks and creaks, they love to hide.
A cat's old yarn, a lazy leap,
Echoes of secrets, never deep.

Chairs creak softly, quite the muse,
With every groan, who can refuse?
The ghosts of laughter linger near,
Stealing glances, full of cheer.

A grumpy gnome, a garden spy,
Lurks behind flowers, oh my, oh my!
Whispers float on gentle breeze,
Tickling noses, bending knees.

A dog that barks at nothing much,
Chasing shadows, quick to clutch.
Every chuckle, a treasure found,
In this jumbled world, joy abounds.

## **A Canvas of Familiar Faces**

Painted in hues so bright,
With grins that could light a room.
Each character's a delight,
They're flowers in full bloom.

There's Grandma with her braid,
And Grandpa with his cheeky grin.
A thousand stories made,
As the chaos began to spin.

The family gathered tight,
With pies stacked high like a dream.
The laughter takes flight,
As the squirrels join the theme.

Each face tells a tale,
Of pranks and wild escapades.
In this world, we set sail,
Riding waves of silly parades.

## Pictures on the Walls of Memory

Snapshots caught in whirls,
Of picnics gone wildly wrong.
With ants in the cake like pearls,
And the frisbee flying along.

Uncle Joe thought he could dance,
With two left feet on the floor.
He twirled like he took a chance,
And knocked over the open door.

A parrot spoke with flair,
Mocking tales from days of yore.
Cracking jokes in mid-air,
Sparking laughter with a roar.

Every frame framed in cheer,
How they evoke hearty delight.
Smiles echo, crystal clear,
As they shimmer in the light.

## Unraveled Threads of Time

Grandma's stories never end,
Of mice that wore fancy shoes.
They'd dance to a tune they'd send,
While sipping on strawberry brews.

A tale of socks that went astray,
Hiding in the couch with glee.
Hilarity chased them away,
To the land of lost laundry.

The old clock ticks in a jest,
It has secrets that it won't tell.
With every chime, we're blessed,
By broken dreams of wishing well.

Days drift like fashion trends,
Each memory a silly hat.
With laughter, time never bends,
As we reminisce of that.

## Fables Spun in Elderberry Hues

Old tales twist like yarn,
Once a cat wore a crown.
He ruled the mice at dawn,
And chased them all around.

Bizarre were the things I'd see,
A grand feast with frogs and bees.
Laughter would echo, oh so free,
As they danced beneath the trees.

A wise old owl took the stage,
With riddles that caused a stir.
The crowd would laugh and engage,
As the punchlines had a blur.

Time stands still in this place,
Stories woven with a grin.
Even the spiders embrace,
A world where no one wears a fin.

## Echoes in the Twilight

Shadows dance as the sun bows low,
Echoes replay all the fun we know.
A kite that flew just a bit too high,
Met with trees and a loud goodbye.

Songs of frogs croak silly rhymes,
As the twilight chimes keep funny times.
Fireflies blink like laughing stars,
Guiding the lost back to their cars.

Once, I aimed an apple to toss,
But hit my brother, oh what a loss!
The laughter that erupted that day,
Still echoes in the funniest way.

In the twilight, we find our place,
In memories wrapped in a giggle embrace.
As night whispers tales of mirth and cheer,
Echoes of laughter draw me near.

## Whispers of Yesteryear

In corners, whispers do parade,
Of stories that never quite fade.
With a chuckle and a nudge, they roam,
Making my heart feel right at home.

The ghost of a sandwich once lost,
Stopped by my table, at what a cost!
It swore it had shimmered in gold,
But alas, kitchen tales grow old.

Old toys have tales beyond the dust,
To pitch a fit, like tiny rust.
They squabble and shout from the shelf,
In language only they can tell.

On rainy days, laughter does brew,
With past mischief that feels brand new.
In whispers that tickle and tease,
Yesteryear's giggles bring me to ease.

## Seasons Enshrined in Stillness


Spring stood with flowers in hand,
While winter threw snow like a band.
Summer pouted, and autumn sighed,
As they each held their secrets inside.

Once, I learned to dance with the leaves,
But tripped and fell, oh what a tease!
The trees all giggled, roots in a knot,
As squirrels took bets on whether I'd flop.

Autumn's grace, a candy parade,
But every sweet treat, soon delayed.
With pumpkins grinning, I lost my way,
Came back with berries, bright and gay.

Seasons giggle, in a merry line,
Whispering jokes about the divine.
In the stillness, they play their game,
A funny dance, never the same.

## The Timekeeper's Gaze

In the corner sits an old clock,
Ticking tales of the silly and mock.
It grins at the socks lost in time,
And laughs at my dance to the rhyme.

The minute hand does a jig,
While memories tap like a pig.
I've tripped over moments once sweet,
Now lie like gum stuck to my feet.

Grandpa's tales about that old cat,
Who swore it could speak like a brat.
The clock chuckled, then half-struck the hour,
As I remembered my childhood power.

Days flew, much like the stork,
Each yet another funny quirk.
With every tick, laughter prevails,
As we spin in our time-travel tales.

## Letters Lost in the Alabaster Dawn


Morning brings its giggles soft,
Letters stuck in the door's fine seam,
As they flutter, we chuckle oft,
Words of silly daydreams and cream.

Ink spills secrets on the ground,
A jam made from thoughts that flee,
As mismatched socks are always found,
In adventures wild, just you and me.

With mismatched paper, we have fun,
Crafting plans beneath the sun,
Tickling thoughts of what's to be,
Lost letters, but our hearts run free.

In every crack, humor speaks,
As the sun's bright laughter here,
Traces of our rosy peaks,
And memories crafted year by year.

## Faded Footprints on the Wooden Plank

Footprints fade on weathered wood,
As we dance in circles wide,
A hop, a skip, oh how we could,
Create a ruckus, stick inside!

Popsicle stains on lazy days,
A treat with every giggling bite,
We laughed and sang in crazy ways,
And turned the wrong way every night.

Old planks echo with our dreams,
Though some were silly, some were grand,
Imagine all our wacky schemes,
From pirate ships to a rock band!

Now as shadows stretch and yawn,
We map the tales of all we've done,
With laughter, hearts will never fawn,
On faded trails, our joy's begun.

## Nostalgia in Every Breeze

A gust of wind steals my hat,
It twirls like a dervish, oh!
Chasing it, I trip and splat—
Leaves laugh as I steal the show!

Whispers from the fence post creak,
Tales of summer's swirling heat,
That time I thought I'd found a creek,
Just a puddle beneath my feet.

Fond memories in the air,
Of lemonade and sun-soaked days,
As grandma's old cat found a chair,
And dared us all to play our ways.

In each breeze, a giggle hides,
Reminders of the fun we had,
While life, like silly string, slides,
Through moments that were just a tad.

## Secrets Beneath the Old Oak

Under branches thick and wide,
Squirrels plot a sneak attack,
On a picnic, we'll decide,
Who will munch a day-old snack.

Raccoons wear their masks with pride,
Sipping soda on the side,
Watch them dance—they're quite the show,
Underneath the old oak's glow.

Laughter echoes, echoes loud,
As the tales of yore unfold,
From silly bets to fireside crowd,
Those moments we can't retold.

The wise old trunk has seen it all,
With bark thicker than our fables,
As we pile our stories tall,
In laughter, life, and kitchen tables.

## Quiet Reflections in a Weathered Chair

In a rickety chair where stories unfold,
Sits a wise old man, but he's mostly bold.
Fingers tapping, he waits for a quip,
With a grin that begs for a silly trip.

Every creak is a giggle, a shout,
From the tales of cats that ran about.
Tea spills a little, just adds to the charm,
Each drop a story, safe from alarm.

Sunset's glow through the slats of the wood,
As he recounts times we all understood.
The chair may be worn, but the laughter is new,
In this quiet refuge, joy's on cue.

## Compositions of a Forgotten Symphony

Rusty keys on a piano grin,
Once struck chords now sing from within.
Cat on the keys, creating a show,
A symphony played by paws, oh, what a flow!

Lost notes flutter like leaves in the breeze,
Tickling our ears with forgotten tease.
Each note whispers tales of the bizarre,
As we chuckle at memories, near and far.

In the shadows, an old music stand sways,
Guarding secrets of melody's plays.
With each plunk from the feline's delight,
We find joy in the echoes of night.

## The Sigh of Settled Dust

Dust bunnies gather, a furry crew,
Each one dreams of a life anew.
Whiskers twitch as they plot for a snack,
But the only thing near is an old knickknack.

Grandma's chair creaks, what a scene,
'It's the dust,' she laughs, 'that keeps me keen!'
Mismatched cushions, and tea stains laugh,
Time whispers secrets in every gaffe.

Worn-out slippers with holes so bold,
Tell tales of legends that never grow old.
As laughter rings in this dust-filled air,
We cherish the moments, nothing to spare.

## Framed Moments in Fading Light

Old photos hang with dusty grace,
Eyes wide in a funny chase.
Grandpa's wig, a fanciful sight,
Caught mid-dance, what a delight!

The cat's in a ludicrous pose,
Chasing shadows, striking a nose.
In laughing frames, time has its say,
Memory plays a comedic play.

Butterfly clips and socks mismatched,
The dog once howled, we all dispatched.
Tickles of joy from years gone by,
In this light, we never say goodbye.

## Illuminated Memories in Twilight

As the sun dips low, stories arise,
With a glint in our eyes, no need for disguise.
Catching fireflies in a jar, what flair!
Each flicker a giggle, hanging in air.

We'd spin daring tales by the light of the moon,
About ghouls and goblins, singing our tune.
But then you asked if the ghost could cook,
And nearly fell off your chair in the nook.

Stars sparkling bright, plot twists await,
You fell for a prank; it was all fate.
A shadowy figure? Just the old cat,
Yet we laughed like mad, 'till we fell flat.

In twilight's embrace, our memories gleam,
Each chuckle and whim, like a silly dream.
Forever etched, this playful glow,
Illuminated laughter in the evening's show.

## Chronicles of a Rustic Existence

Down by the barn, a tale unfolds,
Of chickens plotting, and secrets retold.
One scratched the door, clucked with might,
While we hollered, 'Get back, it's not supper tonight!'

We'd gather the eggs, oh what a stunt,
You victoriously waved, 'I did that front!'
A goat that slipped, a porcupine's hiss,
Each misadventure we couldn't dismiss.

Not a dull day with mud on our shoes,
While dreaming of pizazz in the old news.
Rode off in a cart, made of old wood,
Just like knights charging, it was all good.

All patched and scratched, like our youthful flair,
Every laugh reminding us, life's quite rare.
Hand in hand through fields so vast,
Oh the chronicles of our rustic past!

## Songs Whistled by an Autumn Breeze

Leaves swirling down, a colorful blend,
Each one whispers secrets, legends they send.
The squirrels debate on who'll claim a nut,
While I sit and chuckle at the neighbor's strut.

You wore those socks with such quirky flair,
Mismatched patterns—who did you scare?
We danced through puddles, splashing around,
I soaked your shoes, oh how we both browned!

Falling branches? A game we adored,
Every thump was a laugh or a snore.
When the wind howls, it's just us playing,
On echoes of giggles, we're forever swaying.

With each new gust, memories unfurl,
A whimsical world, oh how we twirl.
Autumn's melody, we'll always cheer,
For laughter and friendship is what brought us here.

## Traces of Love in the Air

Old shoes on the wire, they sway,
Reminds me of cringy dance that day.
You tripped over your own two feet,
And laughed so hard, you fell on the street.

A wink shared under the summer sun,
With ice cream drips, oh what fun!
You thought that you'd be so suave,
But ended up in a sticky grove.

The laughter echoed, carried on breeze,
Our silly fights, like playful tease.
A noodle flicked, right on your head,
Yet still, we giggled till we turned red.

Now sitting here, memories play,
With every chuckle, they never fade away.
Life's a circus, and we were the clowns,
Where joy was found, in laughter we drown.

## When the World Was Slow

When clocks ticked soft and time moved slow,
We chased our shadows, laughing in tow.
Skipping stones, we made them bounce,
Who knew there were just three in counts?

A game of tag through evening glow,
We shouted loud, just to bestow.
The bruised knees, stories of their own,
Gave us the badges we've proudly grown.

The fireflies flickered a dance so bright,
Caught in dreams, we held on tight.
With jelly jars, we'd trap the light,
And release them back, a lively flight!

In days gone by, with laughter loud,
We wove our dreams, both bold and proud.
So let's sit back, reminisce a while,
In humor wrapped, we'll always smile.

## Glimpses of Days Gone By

In sunny glances, shadows play,
Reflecting on our silly day.
A kite got stuck in a tree so tall,
We bottled our giggles, gave it our all!

A picnic spread with ants aplenty,
We feasted well, our laughter hefty.
The sandwich fight was quite the scene,
Mayo splattered on Grandma's green!

The bikes we rode with rusty chains,
Through puddles deep and silly stains.
Each turn and crash a story made,
We'll love those days, they never fade.

So raise a glass, here's to the past,
To friendships strong and moments vast.
With humor bright, and joy as glue,
We'll stitch our memories, tried and true.

## Rustling Leaves and Silent Stories

With rustling leaves, our voices blend,
Each gust of wind brings tales to mend.
A squirrel once stole Grandpa's shoe,
We swear it knew what it would do!

The creaking swing that sways so high,
Carries echoes of our childhood sighs.
"Did I really wear those socks?" we muse,
In stripes so bright we'd surely lose!

The garden gnome with painted grin,
Stood guard through thick and nearly thin.
He winked at us and made a dash,
Living for pranks in a secret stash!

So sit awhile and share the cheer,
Reliving all the joy we hold dear.
With laughter sprouting from our hearts,
We weave the past, and never part.

## **Laughter Softened by Memory**

We gather round with tales to spin,
Of awkward jokes and laughter thin.
The cat, it wore a silly hat,
We still can't figure out just that!

Grandpa's dance was quite a sight,
Two left feet in pure delight.
He tripped and spilled his drink with flair,
We laughed until we gasped for air!

The photo albums, quite a mess,
Each snapshot tells a fun success.
Who knew that Uncle Joe could bake?
A cupcake shaped like a snake!

As memories swirl through autumn's haze,
We chuckle softly, lost in a daze.
For all the years that flew so fast,
We find our joy in the laughter cast.

## Steps Through Time's Garden

With sandals squeaking, we take a stroll,
Through flowerbeds that always stole.
A garden hose, we played like fools,
Making rivers with our own rules.

The gopher peeked, a curious beast,
While we jumped, chasing him in feast.
Marshmallow roasts on nightly camp,
We dodged the smoke from the sluggard lamp.

Countless steps that led to fun,
Every flower danced under the sun.
A paper boat we sent on a quest,
Floated away, but we laughed the best.

So here's to the steps through weeds and blooms,
In playful chaos, laughter looms.
With every skip and hop we find,
A garden of memories, intertwined.

## Shadows of Forgotten Summers

Beneath the sun, we threw our hats,
Shadows stretched like lazy cats.
With popsicle juice down our chins,
We danced to tunes that didn't begin.

A bike with wheels that squeaked and cried,
Raced down the path, with arms open wide.
Each tumble, a giggle, a war of pride,
As we skidded through grass, our time did glide.

Crickets chirped their funny song,
While we debated right from wrong.
Did the neighbor really steal our fries?
Oh, the laughter made us wise!

Now those days are castles in air,
Full of dreams tangled in wild hair.
With every shadow and silly surprise,
We danced beneath the summer skies.

## Memories on the Wind

Whispers of jokes that made us roar,
Echo through the open door.
Tickling winds that tease the mind,
Past silliness we left behind.

The neighbor's cat, a bold little thief,
Raided the fridge without any grief.
We chased it down but laughed too hard,
As it claimed the last hot dog card.

Kites that soared with colors bright,
Tangled up in a tree's great height.
While we stood below in disbelief,
Planning schemes of feline relief.

In every gust, a tickling jest,
A canvas where our joy expresses.
Through breezes that bring a teasing spin,
Our laughing hearts forever win.

# Reflections in Dusty Light

In a chair that creaks and sways,
I ponder on those younger days.
With lemonade and laughter bright,
I miss the way we'd pick a fight.

Old photos stuck in sticky frames,
Show us in our silly games.
The dog wore sunglasses, it's true,
He was the best at hide-and-seek too.

Now I sip my tea and smile,
As memories come back in style.
The fashion back then was quite a sight,
I shudder, but it feels so right.

So come along, let's reminisce,
About the moments we can't miss.
In sunshine, shade, and what's in between,
Laughing at our silly routine.

## Enchanted Echoes of Days Past

In twilight's glow, we recall the sights,
Of roller skates and those silly fights.
With ice cream drips on summer's sweet breeze,
We plotted our conquests among the trees.

Oh, the bicycles, with their rickety wheels,
We'd race like the wind, oh what zest it feels!
But then came the fall, with a belabored din,
Scraped knees and loud yells, we'd still wear a grin.

The treehouse stood proud, a fortress so grand,
Where kingdoms were built by the clumsy hand.
A squirrel, our watchman, with eyes so wise,
Who stole our snacks—a sneaky surprise!

As dusk settles down, with shadowy friends,
We share all our tales, a humor that blends.
With ghosts in the eaves, and laughter afloat,
Memories linger, like an old, funny note.

## Hints of the Celestial in Dusk

The old swing creaks, a ghostly tune,
Whispers float by under silvered moon.
A cat leaps high, in a feathery chase,
While we sip lemonade, laughter's embrace.

Grandma's old tales, with mismatched lore,
Of pirates and dragons, oh what a score!
She swears she saw a UFO land,
But maybe it's just that dust on her hand.

The fireflies dance like they own the night,
Chasing shadows, it's quite the sight.
We're all giving chase, with jars in tow,
Tripping on grass, oh, where did it go?

Then comes the dog with a bark so loud,
He thinks he's a wolf, proud and unbowed.
He chases his tail, the funniest show,
While we laugh till we cry, in the soft glow.

## Heartstrings Tied to Old Lullabies


Nostalgia dances, a waltz in time,
While shadows serenade with a rhyme.
Old lullabies echo, funny and sweet,
As memories line up, each one a treat.

The cat purrs softly, a sleepy bard,
While dreams take flight, though quite a bit charred.
With each note sung, laughter takes wing,
In the heart of the night, joy is the king.

## Hushed Reveries in the Evening Light

In twilight's glow, the stories hum,
A chorus of critters—what's to come?
The old lantern flickers, casting a grin,
As night wraps around, the fun's to begin.

Whispers of the moon, a mischievous sprite,
Tickling secrets in the dead of night.
The stars chuckle, twinkling bright,
As we all slide into sheer delight.

## Sipping Tea with Time's Echo

Teacups clink, laughter spills,
As past and present share their thrills.
A cat dozes, an unwitting star,
While I sip tales from a teapot jar.

Biscuit crumbs and giggles fly,
And ghosts in the corner wink an eye.
Time's echo laughs, it knows the score,
As we spill tea and chase folklore.

## Dappled Light on Weathered Wood

Sunbeams dance on splintered grain,
Old memories chuckle, partly in vain.
A squirrel debates between nuts and cheese,
As shadows giggle in the rustling leaves.

The rocking chair creaks, a wise old sage,
Whispers of stories trapped on the page.
And the breeze, it seems, has jokes to tell,
While birds crack up and handle it well.

## **Mementos Marked in Time**

Old photos grin from a dusty shelf,
Each one a treasure of mischief itself.
Faded laughter spills from each frame,
As we strive to recall every name.

A rusted bike waits for just one more ride,
Its tires are flat, and the seat is wide.
But with a push, we're off in a flash,
Chasing the echoes of each silly crash.

## Dining with the Spirit of the Past

Grandma's recipes, a magical mix,
With secret ingredients and crazy tricks.
The table is set with laughter and cheer,
Though Uncle Bob's still carving the deer.

The vintage chairs creak with stories to tell,
As flying peas start their own choral spell.
A turkey wobbles, its fate in the air,
While kids plot schemes without a care.

## Afterglow of Lasting Moments

A garden gnome in a sun hat grins,
He's been there through thick and all our sins.
Recounting tales of the way things were,
As butterflies venture without a stir.

The swing set squeaks like old-fashioned tunes,
While shadows stretch like weary raccoons.
A kite once flew, now tangled in a tree,
It giggles low with every passing breeze.

## Visions of a Gentle Yesterday

Old hats hang low, a silly sight,
With mismatched socks, oh what a fright.
The cat wore glasses, all dressed for tea,
As memories danced like bees in a spree.

Lawn chairs creaked with laughter's sound,
Collective sighs from the folks around.
A pie was baked but it rolled away,
Chasing the dog who thought it was play.

Original title:
The Porch of the Past

Copyright © 2025 Creative Arts Management OÜ
All rights reserved.

Author: Alec Donovan
ISBN HARDBACK: 978-1-80587-217-7
ISBN PAPERBACK: 978-1-80587-687-8

www.ingramcontent.com/pod-product-compliance
Lightning Source LLC
Chambersburg PA
CBHW060134230426
43661CB00003B/420